Original title:
Life's Big Mysteries Solved (Sort Of)

Copyright © 2025 Creative Arts Management OÜ
All rights reserved.

Author: Lucas Harrington
ISBN HARDBACK: 978-1-80566-173-3
ISBN PAPERBACK: 978-1-80566-468-0

Echoes of Unspoken Truths

Why do socks disappear in wash?
They take a vacation, oh what a frosh.
Left to ponder their life so grand,
In the land of lint, they make a stand.

Do cats know something we don't?
With their mysterious glances, they flaunt.
Are they plotting or just bored with us?
A feline conspiracy, quite a fuss!

The Map to Nowhere

Found a map marked with an X,
Turns out it's just for junk food specs.
Pizza places, fries in a row,
Adventure is really just a food show.

GPS lost, can't find the way,
Detours lead us to a buffet.
Every wrong turn is a tasty find,
Turns out wandering's truly divine!

Unlocking the Veil of Ordinary

Why does cereal float like a dream?
Perhaps they're training for a team.
Swimming through milk, doing the backstroke,
Breakfast athletes? That's not a joke!

The allure of Tupperware lids,
Why's it a puzzle? It tops all bids.
Every cupboard an unmade bed,
In search of order, but chaos instead!

Illuminated Questions at Midnight

Why does ice cream always melt fast?
It knows our love and can't last.
Beneath the stars, we ponder and sigh,
Will my midnight snack simply say goodbye?

Why does the light bulb flicker late?
It's debating whether to get a date.
Each pop and buzz a silent scream,
Maybe it needs a restful dream!

The Hunt for Clarity in Chaos

In a world so wild, I search for clues,
With a magnifying glass, I sip my brews.
Finding meaning in socks that don't match,
Is it fashion or chaos? A puzzling scratch!

Navigating through life's jumbled heap,
Like counting the sheep, I struggle to sleep.
Each answer I seek slips out of reach,
Maybe the truths are just lessons to teach.

Illusions of Certainty

So sure I was, on a path divine,
A map in my pocket, everything aligned.
But every turn led to yet another twist,
Turns out the map's just a foggy mist!

I asked a wise man, 'What's the key?'
He shrugged and said, 'Just let it be!'
So I danced in circles, my head in a spin,
Finding certainty feels like a playful sin.

Flickers of Insight in Darkness

In the shadowy corners of my mind's maze,
A flicker of insight induces a craze.
I stumble on thoughts, like tripping on stairs,
The answers are near, but where are the pairs?

With a light bulb above, I clumsily grin,
Is this genius or just a whimsical spin?
Eureka rings out as I giggle in fright,
That maybe the darkness knows more than the light.

The Delicate Balance of Wonder

Between awe and confusion, there lies a dance,
Like socks and sandals, what's the chance?
Balancing wonder with a chuckle or two,
What a sight, this odd world, it's all askew!

I marvel at rainbows, then trip on a shoe,
With each twist and turn, I find something new.
Laughter erupts, my joy starts to sway,
In this delicate balance, I happily play.

The Intangible Threads

We ponder where socks always flee,
Is there a cosmic laundry spree?
They vanish without a single cue,
Just like my will to eat tofu.

Are there gnomes living under my bed?
Or just dust bunnies, long overdue?
Their giggles echo in the night,
As I search for my missing shoe.

We wonder why cats rule the world,
With their soft paws and tails unfurled.
Is it a charm or magic spell?
Maybe they just do it for the gel.

So let's embrace these silly thoughts,
And see what fun the mystery brought.
For in this laughable little course,
We find humor, and that's the source.

Embracing the Unknown Journey

Where do lost keys wander away?
Is there a party we can't sway?
They leave us with locked doors each night,
A mystery craving insight.

What about the food left on plates?
Do they plot their own escape dates?
They shrink as we're served at the table,
Rebels of dinner, quite unstable.

Do vegetables have secret lives?
Conspiring when the fridge door dives?
I swear, they laugh when I'm not there,
While plotting schemes with the cold air.

Let's cherish these quirky conundrums,
As we spin through life's random rhythms.
For every path we take on our ride,
Is peppered with giggles we can't hide.

Final Questions over First Answers

Why does the toast always land down?
Is that a symbol of fate's own crown?
Each breakfast feels like a grand debate,
As crumbs await a toast-based fate.

What's with the socks turning into pets?
Do they plot over coffee and sets?
They rearrange every time I'm gone,
Are they putting on a sock-based con?

Do we really need that extra slice?
Or is it just life being nice?
With crumbs of joy and hints of glee,
That slice knows it's meant to be free.

Let's laugh at these questions profound,
For wisdom often rolls on the ground.
In these riddles, we find our cheer,
And dance with the mysteries year after year.

Queries of the Heart and Mind

Why do socks disappear in the wash?
Is it for freedom or just a big nosh?
And what makes cats plot their attacks?
Searching for answers, we just face the facts.

Why does chocolate taste like a dream?
Especially when paired with ice cream?
And why do we laugh when things go wrong?
Perhaps that's where the heart feels strong.

Threads of Insight

Why do we crave what we can't quite get?
Is it fate calling, or just a safe bet?
Do we dance for joy or to hide the gloom?
Sometimes it's hard to know where to zoom.

When did wearing pants become a requirement?
In a world full of clothes, is that alignment?
And why do we sing out of tune with glee?
Perhaps it's just part of being free!

When Certainty Meets Curiosity

Do aliens laugh at our funky ways?
Or do they just watch us in a daze?
What's with the traffic lights—red, green, and gold?
Turns out it's just a story retold.

Why do we fear what we can't see?
Is it shadows lurking or just old debris?
And how come every time we try to be cool,
We just end up looking like a silly fool?

The Riddles We Embrace

What's the secret of the perfect nap?
Is it taught in schools or just a mishap?
Why do we giggle at things that confound?
In laughter's echo, the truth can be found.

How does a pillow know just how to hug?
It's soft and cuddly, like a warm bug.
And why is the sky so blue and wide?
Does it hide its secrets, somewhere inside?

Whispers of the Unanswered

Why do socks disappear, so sly?
A dryer gremlin? Oh my, oh my!
They vanish quick, without a trace,
Leaving one lone sock in its place.

And where does all the missing pens go?
They slip away, with a quiet flow.
Maybe they're writing tales unknown,
Living wild lives, now on their own.

What's the point of left and right?
Why is it always a wrestling fight?
When trying to choose which way to steer,
It feels like directions vanished in the air.

Do dreams have a secret book to keep?
With tales so silly, they make you weep?
I'd love to read what's in that tome,
But waking up means I'm back at home.

Shadows of Familiar Faces

Is that a friend or a stranger near?
That blurry glance fills me with fear.
Do I wave, or keep my gaze low?
The mystery thickens, it's quite the show.

Why are cats always plotting at night?
With their sneaky paws and a beady sight,
Are they solving puzzles of cosmic rate,
Or just looking for the perfect plate?

Why does ice cream melt when it's hot?
A sticky mess is what I've got.
What if love's the answer to why?
But it's just a scoop, a sweetened lie.

Why do my plants always seem to die?
I water them well, yet they sigh and lie.
Maybe they plot garden rebellions,
Conspiring with weeds under the pavilions.

The Enigma of Everyday Wonders

What's the deal with elevator music?
It's soothing, yet feels a bit too cryptic.
Why do we sway in a quiet trance?
As a tune leads us to an awkward dance.

Who's counting calories, anyway?
That slice of cake calls out to play.
A bite here, a nibble there,
Lost count again, need a fresh air affair!

Why do we park in spaces unclear?
Like a game of Twister! Oh dear, oh dear!
One wheel on a line, the other way out,
Conversations of chaos without a doubt.

What's the mystery of cereal and milk?
A breakfast duo, as soft as silk.
Do they gossip when we're not around?
Crunching secrets without a sound.

Clues in the Coffee Grounds

Why does morning coffee call my name?
It brews me strength, I can't complain.
But what's the magic behind that cup?
It lifts me high, then makes me jump!

Do coffee beans have secrets to share?
They whisper warmth in the morning air.
What tales unfold as I sip away?
Mysteries brewed, come what may!

Why does each spill feel like a crime?
A splash of brown at the worst of times.
Is it a sign? A message profound?
Or just my luck turning around?

Where does the cream go when it swirls?
In a dance with the coffee, it twirls.
Is there a party in the mug so deep?
Or just my caffeine dreams, too sweet to keep?

Between Clue and Confusion

I lost my keys by the door,
I checked the fridge, and then the floor.
Mysterious socks in a lonely pile,
Where logic and chaos meet in style.

The cat just stares, like a sage,
While I flip through this mental page.
A puzzle assembled from random bits,
Turns out it's just my missed appointments!

The Web of Mystique

In the attic, a box of dust,
Where secrets linger, and shadows bust.
My grandma's hat, a crown of lore,
How did it end up beside the floor?

The squirrels conspire on my roof,
While I wonder, was that a hoof?
Mystique woven in bramble and string,
And all I ask is 'What did you bring?'

Ephemeral Glimpses

Life rushes by, a fleeting show,
Like the last slice of pizza, it goes, you know?
Picnic ants march in a grand parade,
While I ponder my lemonade cascade.

Moments flicker like a broken light,
Do I chase them? Or just take flight?
My mind's a circus—what a delight!
In a world so strange, I dance with fright.

Wondering Through Ambiguity

A road less traveled leads me here,
Where logic fades and jokes appear.
Why's my coffee cold, yet so divine?
Is it magic, or just bad design?

The clock ticks loud, it laughs at time,
While I try to muster a witty rhyme.
Confusion reigns like a carnival ride,
So I hop on board, and enjoy the glide.

Shadows of Understanding

What's the deal with socks that stray?
They vanish, like ghosts in the fray.
The cat's the suspect, I suspect,
With his knowing grin, oh so direct.

Why do we ponder the stars above?
When pizza delivers the truth we love?
We play at guessing the universe wide,
While munching on snacks, with crumbs at our side.

The Great Puzzle of Existence

A jigsaw with pieces that somehow fit,
But one's swollen—what a strange bit!
A corner piece from a puzzle of yore,
   Does it belong, or is there more?

Why do we wonder what lies out of reach?
When ice cream's the lesson, it's soft, not a speech.
Grains of sand in the hourglass sway,
   Yet here sits my cone, so sweet on a tray.

Echoes of the Unexplainable

Why does the toaster burn, oh why?
With a crumb on top and a sad good-bye.
The coffee mug laughs as I try to pour,
Pathways of caffeine behind each door.

Voices of echoes, they bounce and they play,
While I search for meaning in yesterday's clay.
A dance of the crazy, a waltz of the wild,
Am I the adult, or am I the child?

Unlocking the Veil of Reality

The fridge hums secrets in the night,
It guards our snacks, oh what a sight!
Peeking slyly, it knows it's true,
The cake of mystery—dare I pursue?

Life's got riddles, like socks with no mates,
But laughter's the key that negotiates.
Unlocking the door with a chuckle and grin,
Perhaps the answers are where we begin.

Visions of Unclarity

I saw a cat wearing a tie,
Asking the fish why they fly.
The fish just blinked, looked a bit lost,
Wondering what's next, at what cost.

A frog in a hat croaks a tune,
While dancing under the bright moon.
He said, "Let's chat about the stars!"
But all I got were golf ball scars.

The Heartbeats of Enigma

A squirrel debated the meaning of nuts,
With a wise old owl in a pair of struts.
The owl just hooted, 'What's the big deal?'
'It's all just fluff, let's spin the wheel!'

A tree told a joke, the wind was the punch,
And everyone laughed as they sat down to munch.
Mysteries grow like weeds in the yard,
But I still can't find my lost credit card.

The Calm of the Unanswered

Why does my toast always land face down?
Is the universe playing, throwing my frown?
A butterfly giggled while sipping some tea,
Saying, "Who knows? Just dance with glee!"

A penguin proposed, 'Let's question the ice,'
But all the seals just rolled, 'Not so nice!'
Inquiries swirl like leaves in a breeze,
Yet answers evade like the neighbor's keys.

Curiosities We Have Yet to Understand

I asked my goldfish about the moon,
He winked at me, then hummed a tune.
Is he a scholar in cosmic lore?
Or just always hungry for food galore?

What's your favorite flavor, oh wise vacuum?
It hummed back softly, 'I like a good boom!'
They say questions can lead to great things,
But sometimes they just flop like broken wings.

The Path of Questions

Why do socks disappear, so sly?
A sneaky plot, or just a lie?
The missing spoon, where did it go?
It vanished fast, like my last dough.

Why do cats sit high on the shelf?
Do they ponder deeply, or just themselves?
What's in their minds, a grand parade?
Or just a nap in sun, nicely laid.

A Journey into the Uncharted

What's the flavor of a rainbow's arc?
Sweet as a laugh or bright as a spark?
Do dreams come true in the light of day?
Or are they just clouds that faded away?

If time travels forward, where's the rear?
Do we leave behind our hopes and cheer?
If wishes were fish, would oceans be full?
Or just empty nets, with minds that pull?

The Kaleidoscope of Reality

Why does life twist and turn like a dance?
In a whirl of color, we take a chance.
Do mirrors reflect what we truly are?
Or just jumbled images, near and far?

Is cereal soup? A breakfast debate?
With rules of the game, we negotiate.
In this jumble, we laugh and we sigh,
As questions of food make our spirits fly.

Half-Answers and Full Hearts

Why does laughter bubble up like tea?
A mystery brewed in camaraderie.
Do hugs hold answers to what we seek?
Or just warmth and joy, week after week?

If the moon winks down from the sky,
Is it teasing us, oh my, oh my?
In every puzzle, a giggle unfolds,
For half the answer is worth its gold.

Glances into the Beyond

Why do socks disappear,
In the wash they take flight?
One day they were here,
Now just an empty sight.

Do fish ever get thirsty?
Do trees ever get sad?
Is the moon just a disk,
That plays tricks on the glad?

Why does pizza taste better,
At midnight in dim light?
It's a culinary thriller,
A gourmet delight!

What happened to the whispers,
That danced in the breeze?
Are they hiding in shadows,
Or roaming with ease?

Questioning the Known

What makes toast so crispy,
But bread soft as a cloud?
Is there a toast fairy,
That makes breakfast proud?

Why does ice cream melt,
On hot summer's embrace?
Is it sneaking away,
From the heat's warm face?

Do cats have secret lives,
When humans are not there?
Are they plotting world peace,
Or just taking a hair?

What's the deal with the stars,
Do they twinkle on cue?
Or are they winking at us,
With a galactic crew?

Treading Water in the Deep

Why do we fear the dark,
Yet crave shadows at night?
Is there comfort in secrets,
Whispered out of sight?

Why do we laugh at ghosts,
Yet jump at every sound?
Is it humor or horror,
In the fear we have found?

When we swim in the deep,
Do the fish share our plight?
Are they treading their waters,
With unlike delight?

How come owls are wise,
And yet make no good friends?
Is it the glasses they wear,
Or their nocturnal trends?

The Silence of Answers

What does silence really mean,
Does it hum or just sigh?
Is it the pause of thought,
Or a whisper gone by?

Why do the answers hide,
Behind a curtain of doubt?
Is it fun to play games,
And make us figure out?

Do clouds feel the weight,
Of the thoughts flying high?
Or do they just float along,
With no reason to try?

What's up with the sunrise,
Is it painting the sky?
Or just throwing a party,
When darkness says goodbye?

The Horizon of Possibilities

Why do socks vanish in the wash?
Are they off to dance with the stars?
A mystery wrapped in fabric and fluff,
Leaving us with mismatched memoirs.

Do birds gossip about our choices?
Are they plotting from their lofty perch?
Watching us stumble, like little boys,
While they gossip from tree branches' search.

What about the food that goes missing?
Did it dream of a journey afar?
Hidden in plain sight, like a magician,
With leftovers that turned into spar.

Questions like these keep us awake,
Yet laughter is our little clue!
For in this wild journey we take,
The unknown is always our view.

When Awareness Meets Wonder

What's the reason behind all the puns?
Is there logic in laughter's embrace?
Or do words just get tangled for fun,
    Like socks in a chaotic race?

Why do we giggle at silly things?
Is it joy that we find in despair?
Laughter's the melody that life sings,
    Making sense of the oddities rare.

Do clouds have dreams of exploring?
Do they wish to see what lies below?
Or are they just floating, ignoring,
    The two-headed fish that likes to show?

When wonder and wits collide with noise,
    The universe chuckles right back.
For insight is wrapped in silly joys,
    And it's humor that keeps us on track.

Shadows and Sunlight

What's the secret to a shadow's dance?
Do they play with the sunlight's glow?
Or is it a quirky game of chance,
A twirl that they want us to know?

Why do you trip over invisible things?
Is there a gremlin playing its tricks?
Or perhaps the world just has silly flings,
Creating those wobbly sticks?

Do you think mirrors have feelings too?
Staring back, does it ever question?
Is it just reflecting the self-debauchery,
Or plotting a weird intervention?

In shadows and sunlight we find our way,
Both unwitting comedy stunts on display.
As we chase the mysteries night and day,
Let's laugh at the quirkiness on the way.

The Art of Not Knowing

Why do we forget names in a flash?
Is it a mental game on repeat?
Like a runaway train on a crazy crash,
Chasing the remnants of our fleeting greet?

What's up with dreams that make no sense?
Do they laugh at us in the night?
A carnival ride of whimsical suspense,
Leaving us blank at morning light?

Is there wisdom in the fool's parade?
And do they teach secrets of the wise?
Or is it the joy that's never repaid,
That spins in a circle, just to surprise?

For in the art of not knowing it seems,
Lies the laughter and joy of the jest.
With questions that bumble into our dreams,
We dance through the chaos and jest.

Reflections in a Broken Mirror

I looked in the glass but saw my cat,
She winked and then pounced on a mat.
I sighed and straightened my hair with care,
Only to find a pancake stuck there.

The cracks told tales of pies and snacks,
Of late-night snacks and silly hacks.
Each shard revealed a funny face,
Of my neighbor's dog that stole my space.

In pieces, reflections danced with glee,
Each glimmer sparked a new comedy.
Who knew my mirror, once so pristine,
Could turn daydreams into a funny scene?

So here's to the cracks and what they show,
A squashed banana or a toe-to-toe.
In a world that's oft too serious,
A broken mirror seems quite curious.

The Story Beneath the Surface.

Beneath the waters, fish do laugh,
Their jokes, a slippery, gleeful graft.
One finny fellow told a tall tale,
Of a crab who wore a tiny veil.

The secrets of pond life, oh so clear,
With frogs that joke in a croaky cheer.
But when I asked for the grand reveal,
A turtle whispered, "Let's keep it real."

They swam in circles, circling the point,
While turtles twiddled their finny joint.
The depth of mysteries, wide and deep,
Yet still they tease me, no secrets to keep.

So I chuckled, splashed in the goo,
For under the surface, fun's never through.
Lessons in humor, the best of swim,
In murky waters, all tales are grim.

The Secrets We Unravel

In a box of socks, I found a shoe,
And a forgotten note that simply said, 'Boo!'
The secrets were tangled in wool and lace,
Of oddities that never found their place.

I opened a drawer, caught a whiff of cheese,
Just beneath the papers, among the keys.
What mysteries lie in basement gloom?
I laughed to find a gnome with a broom!

The cat joined in, with a flip of her tail,
She wove through stories, leaving a trail.
We giggled at fantasy, strange and bizarre,
As my mismatched socks danced like a star.

So here's to the laughter in each hidden nook,
For every secret holds a funny hook.
In unraveling life, we find a big grin,
In the oddest of places, we chuckle within.

In Search of Hidden Truths

I searched for answers in my garden wide,
Then tripped on the hose and fell aside.
A worm looked up with a wiggly grin,
"You'll never find truth where mud has been!"

I peered in flowers, expected to see,
A wise old sage or a bumblebee.
Instead, a daisy shouted, 'Just laugh, dear!'
And a snail said, 'Truth is often mere fear!'

I chased a squirrel who claimed he knew,
Of wisdom found in a burrow or two.
But he just stole my sandwich and ran,
Leaving me with crumbs, the perfect plan!

So I learned that seeking can lead to a plight,
Yet humor can turn the wrong into right.
In search of the hidden, I came up with glee,
For laughter's the truth that sets us all free.

Songs of the Unsolved

A sock's true partner goes unseen,
Yet we wash in pairs, a funny routine.
The toaster hates a buttered slice,
As crumbs rain down, it's not so nice.

Why do we talk to our plants with care?
Do they listen? Do they even care?
In the fruit bowl, ripe bananas plead,
'Why us first? This isn't our creed!'

What makes the cat knock things off the shelf?
Is it for fun or just for itself?
We laugh at puzzles that fill our nights,
Like why the moon's so good at moonlit fights.

Portraits of the Unseen

Invisible friends in our childhood dreams,
Where giggles and whispers swirl in moonbeams.
Mismatched socks dance on laundry day,
In the land of the lost, they frolic and play.

The squirrels have secrets, they chat with glee,
As they plot world domination, you see!
Who knew that life came with such odd twists?
Look out for the dangers of lavender mist!

Why do we chase down the ice cream truck's song?
But end up with flavors that feel so wrong?
Oh, snapshots of moments that make us chuckle,
Captured beside that three-legged buckle.

The Quest for Meaning Beyond Words

We wrote a book on pondering time,
Yet its title feels like a nursery rhyme.
Why do we ponder what cookies are baked?
Is it the crunch, or the crumbs that we make?

The quest for truth leads us in circles,
While coffee spills over our life's big hurdles.
What is the meaning of a floating balloon?
Is it freedom or just a big summer swoon?

We giggle at thoughts that race through our heads,
Like why are we sleepy after sipping our meds?
The answers remain as elusive as air,
Yet we'll keep searching without a care.

Threads of Connection and Confusion

Why do we step on gum with such grace?
Only to find it's stuck to our face.
The cat brings us gifts as if we're in debt,
Like opened cans make us the pet vet!

We text our friends without any words,
Just emojis of cats and a flock of birds.
The WiFi's a ghost, it fizzles and fades,
Yet our love for memes never invades.

Connected like wires, confused like a desk,
In this world of chaos, is it all too grotesque?
We laugh at our blunders, with no fear of crime,
Just chasing the answers through giggles and rhyme.

Whispers of the Unknown

In the fridge lies a fruit, a mystery bright,
A mango or a kiwi? The choice isn't right.
Is it ripe? Is it time? The clock starts to chime,
I ponder these questions, like they're life's paradigm.

Under the bed, dust bunnies do hide,
With secrets they keep, and courage denied.
Are they planning a coup? Or just gathering fluff?
The questions linger on, like old coffee stuff.

The socks in the dryer, they vanish so fast,
A phenomenon puzzling, I've yet to outlast.
Do they dance with the lint? Or off to a world,
Where matching socks wander, their fabric unfurled?

A sock that was striped, now might come back blue,
Like a riddle wrapped tight, just like a bad stew.
So here's to the quirks and laughs that we find,
In every odd corner, a truth's intertwined.

The Enigma of Everyday

Why do chairs always seem to hold my keys?
Like they're plotting against me, if you please.
Every time I sit, mischief is their goal,
I leave with a chuckle, then lose my control.

The toaster's a magician, always a joke,
Burnt toast on the floor, whose skill is this poke?
Breakfast surprises that give quite a fright,
Like breakfast in the dark, in the dead of night.

Refrigerators hum, with a tune so sweet,
Yet when I'm alone, their rhythms retreat.
They love to gossip, with whispers and sighs,
As leftovers cringe in their spacious disguise.

From the coffee pot's gurgle to the cat's sly prance,
Everyday objects invite us to dance.
So let's sip and smile, in this thing we call life,
Embrace every laugh, amidst all the strife.

Lessons from the Unseen

The bathroom mirror shows a face that seems new,
Every morning's a mystery; who are you?
With toothpaste like art, a masterpiece bold,
Reflecting on dreams that have yet to be told.

Yet in the quiet night, shadows come alive,
With squeaks and odd noises, they jive and thrive.
Are they here to teach me, a lesson profound?
Or just to confuse me, without making a sound?

The plants grow so slowly, yet who's watching them?
They whisper sweet secrets, in the quietest hem.
A leaf, it just smiles, soaking up all the rays,
While I scratch my head, lost in nature's maze.

A fork in the drawer, a spoon with a friend,
Their chatter contagious, like stories they send.
In lessons untaught, we find laughter anew,
From the ordinary trinkets, wisdom shines through.

Clues Beneath the Surface

Underneath my garden, the worms plot away,
Digging grand tunnels for a future ballet.
What choreography lies in the ground?
Or are they just laughing, without making a sound?

A potted plant whispers of secrets held tight,
It sways in the breeze, but travels no flight.
With roots deep in soil, it dreams of the sun,
Where does it wander, when day's almost done?

The old oak tree stands with its branches stretched wide,
It's seen every laugh, every tear that we hide.
What tales does it keep, in the rustling leaves?
Each rustle a clue, as the wind softly weaves.

From puddles of mystery, to shadows that play,
There's laughter in questions that won't go away.
So let's ponder and giggle at life's funny clues,
For beneath all the chaos, we've nothing to lose.

Mapping the Maze of Thought

In a world where thoughts collide,
A cat thinks it's God, not some guide.
With socks that disappear, oh so sly,
    Is it a mystery or just a lie?

We navigate through screens and memes,
    Chasing wandering, bizarre dreams.
    Is there a manual for this race?
    Or is it just a wild goose chase?

With lists and notes that pile up high,
Did I write down lunch, or just goodbye?
The mind's a maze we wander through,
    Searching for clues, just me and you.

So here's to chaos that feels so grand,
With mismatched socks, we boldly stand.
Together we'll laugh, let out a cheer,
For solving thoughts, at least we're near!

The Puzzle of Seconds

Seconds ticking, a riddle in time,
Why's morning coffee always a crime?
At two in the morn, I ponder my fate,
Did I finish my snacks, or await?

The clock says it's noon, I'm still in bed,
Is it lunch or just dreams in my head?
Why does time fly, then crawl like a snail?
Each minute a puzzle, each tick a tale.

I lost track again of what I should do,
Chasing those moments like kittens at play.
Are seconds elusive, or trying to tease?
Maybe they're playing hide and seek with ease.

But here's to the puzzle, the joys it imparts,
As we trip through existence with wide open hearts.
Each fleeting second's a laugh or a sigh,
So raise your glasses, let's not let them fly!

Mysteries in the Mundane

What's in the fridge, a culinary quest?
Last night's dinner or a strange fest?
Tupperware's clingy, it holds its own fate,
Is it spaghetti, or just a debate?

Pants missing pockets could lead to despair,
Where did it go, the piece of my pair?
Is there a portal for keys I can find?
Or is it just chaos, a prank on my mind?

The laundry's a whirlpool of colors and fluff,
One sock wanders, the rest gather tough.
Are they conspiring to flee far away?
With secrets untold, they won't let me stay.

So let's laugh at the quirks in our day,
As we chase the mundane that gets in the way.
Each mishap a mystery, a giggle or glee,
In the puzzle of normal, just you and me!

Shattered Facades and Hidden Paths

Behind the curtain, what do we see?
Just a collection of cats drinking tea.
With glittering smiles, we step on the stage,
But the real show's the cat in a rage.

The grass is always greener, or so they say,
But it hides a world of mulch and decay.
Underneath the surface, the truth colors fade,
Like broccoli masquerading as a cascade.

We wear our masks like a funny disguise,
Yet laugh at the truth that bubbles and pries.
With paths winding left, and then right,
Do you follow the signs, or let them take flight?

So let's twist our tales with humor and cheer,
Celebrate puzzles that stem from our fear.
With shattered facades, we dance with a grin,
For the hidden paths always lead back to kin!

In the Fog of Knowing

In the fog where secrets swim,
We ponder truths, on a whim.
A squirrel whispers, 'What's the point?'
As we search for clues, but miss the joint.

A plate of pasta, twirled with glee,
Asking us, 'Are you really free?'
The noodles giggle, slippery fate,
While we just wonder, contemplate.

Aliens chuckle, from afar,
'You humans think you're such a star.'
With each new riddle, we just play,
In this fog, we dance and sway.

In the end, it's all a joke,
As we try to solve what's smoke.
Here's a riddle, just for fun,
Why chase wisdom when you can run?

The Mystery of Every Breath

Each breath we take, a quirky feat,
Floating on air, quite a treat.
Why do we breathe, in and out?
Is it just to stay without doubt?

A goldfish gasps, and I just sigh,
He'll never know the reason why.
Why is it we ponder so deep?
Maybe it's just to stay awake from sleep.

With every inhale, a wild guess,
Are we just here to make a mess?
The question lingers, out we go,
Chasing phantoms while breathing slow.

Yet in the chaos, we find our place,
In every breath, a gentle grace.
After all, what's really the need,
If laughter's our finest breed?

An Odyssey of Unseen Paths

Down winding roads of muddled thought,
We tread on paths that may be caught.
Is it the weather that bends our way?
Or perhaps it's just the game we play?

A cat on a fence, plotting its course,
Scoffs at our worries with feline force.
Each step we take, a curious spin,
Wondering where the journey will begin.

With tangled maps and lost directions,
We frolic blindly, no real corrections.
Each misstep is just a detour,
Another reason to laugh, for sure.

In this journey that seems absurd,
We're all just players, haven't you heard?
So let's embrace the fun and cheer,
For unseen paths lead us right here.

The Intersection of Thought and Wonder

At the corner of thought and surprise,
Thoughts dance around, a bit of a guise.
Curiosity winks, as we ponder and twirl,
In this whimsical realm, we spin and we whirl.

A clock ticks softly, mocking our haste,
'Why rush through this? You'll miss the taste!'
A donut grins, as if to convey,
The secret to joy is in every cliché.

While pondering why socks often stray,
And if ducks ever plan their getaway,
We giggle softly, at riddles so grand,
The intersection's where we make our stand.

As thoughts collide with wonderous flair,
We realize the magic lives everywhere.
So raise a toast to the strange and absurd,
In laughs and whispers, let joy be heard.

When Shadows Speak

Shadows whisper in the night,
Secrets lost in fuzzy light.
Why do they dance, then slip away?
Are they just ghosts on holiday?

They stretch and yawn, take quirky shapes,
Mimic our moves, as if on tapes.
Can they tell a joke or two?
Or just watch us like a morning dew?

Under the glow of the moon's kind eye,
Shadows giggle, never shy.
Is their laughter deep or shallow?
Guessing their thoughts feels like a hello.

So next time you feel their chilly tickle,
Remember, dear friend, they're only a giggle.
Crack a smile, don't take it to heart,
For shadows know how to play their part.

On the Brink of Epiphany

Standing on thoughts that wobble and sway,
Searching for answers, come what may.
Why do socks vanish in the wash?
Do they elope, or is it a posh?

My mind's a labyrinth, twist and turn,
Each corner reveals new things to discern.
Like why do cats plot world domination?
Is it simply a feline fascination?

A flash of brilliance may spark just then,
Only to fizzle, as quick as a pen.
What if the wisdom's not quite profound?
Just a leftover thought, lost and bound?

So laugh at the questions, embrace the jest,
For every mishap, we're simply blessed.
Let epiphanies dance on the edge,
And giggle at truths we'll never hedge.

The Nature of Queries

In a world filled with puzzling stuff,
Why's the simple never enough?
Questions tumble, like marbles they roll,
What's the shortcut to find your soul?

Do ducks ever ponder their quacky scheme?
Or is it just part of the water dream?
Why do we wonder, over and again,
Is it a hobby or just our zen?

Ask the fridge where it has been,
It hums a tune, but doesn't come clean.
Can veggies really sing a refrain?
Or do they giggle at our mundane pain?

So let's toss questions in a playful spree,
Like confetti floating, wild and free.
Adventures await, with each silly probe,
In the grand cosmos, we're all part of the globe.

Chasing Glimmers of Meaning

Glimmers hidden beneath the bed,
What is it hiding? A snack or dread?
Chasing sparkles like they're rare gold,
But only find dust bunnies very bold.

Are oranges really just round bursts of joy?
Or a citrus plot with a playful ploy?
Laughing at labels the world has packed,
What does it mean when your shoe is whacked?

The cat sits smug; he knows a lot,
While we stumble through puzzles, lost in thought.
Is the cheese in the fridge just plain or divine?
Maybe it's lurking, keeping in line.

So let's chase glimmers with all our might,
Even if they flitter, out of sight.
In the end, it's the chase that's most fun,
And learning to laugh is the number one.

Skimming the Surface of Truth

Beneath the waves, the truth may hide,
But look too close, and you might slide.
A dolphin laughs, a seal does dance,
While fish ask, 'Is this your best chance?'

Rubber ducks float in a sea of thought,
Each quack a question, each splash a plot.
The bottom's murky, or so they say,
But who'd dive deep on a sunny day?

A lighthouse beams, a sailor sighs,
Is that a beacon, or just more lies?
They check their compasses, spin around,
As jellyfish giggle, all safe and sound.

So let's play tag with confusion's grace,
Waltz on the waves in a charming chase.
For here on the surface, we just might find,
That laughter's where the truth's aligned.

Ponderings on the Edge

Perched on the brink, with snacks in tow,
Life's quirkiness starts to show.
A squirrel debates, should it take the leap?
But it won't, of course; it's way too cheap.

Why do we worry, hate or pine?
When the universe just wants to dine?
A cosmic joke, they're laughing wide,
As we sweat the small stuff, feeling fried.

Infinity's vast, yet here we are,
Counting shoes, and our favorite car.
With ducks on the pond playing chess,
Do I ponder too much, or just digress?

So here's to the edge, the fun we find,
In every riddle, our hearts unwind.
Let's sip our drinks and toast the night,
To questions that dance just out of sight.

Fables of the Forgotten

In a land where socks disappear,
The tales are strange but bring good cheer.
A king was crowned with a hat made of cheese,
While mice plotted revolts with relative ease.

A dragon sells insurance, quite robust,
In a cave filled with treasures, just gather dust.
Unicorns flit with a hint of sass,
Holding court in the grass as they pass.

Old folks tell yarns of the golden past,
While the present dances around so fast.
If only we could glean some wisdom,
From the mythic errors of a lost kingdom.

So gather 'round, leave your worries at hand,
For fables are fun in this quirky land.
And whether they're true or just in our heads,
We'll laugh at the nonsense the wise folk said.

Gazing into the Abyss

Peering deep into the starry dark,
We see strange things that leave a mark.
Like socks, missing, in the cosmic abyss,
Or why the cat always lands amiss.

The void whispers secrets, but shush, be coy,
For it has a sense of humor, oh what a joy!
Is that black hole a portal, or just an old tire?
With galaxies giggling, they'll never retire.

Time's just a noodle, all twisted and bent,
Do we measure smiles or hours spent?
In this sphere of wonder, let's skip and trample,
Dancing with stardust as time does a scramble.

So peep into the abyss, don't be uptight,
Wink at the mysteries, they're a delightful sight.
For in a universe vast and absurdly grand,
Who needs the answers when you have a band?

Secrets Beneath the Surface

Why do socks vanish in the wash?
Are they off on some grand trip?
Or perhaps they're plotting a heist,
In the dryer they silently slip.

The fridge hums a sophisticated tune,
While leftovers plot their escape.
Do they wish to join the cosmic dance?
Or just dream of a new shape?

Every cat seems to have a plan,
With whiskers twitching in delight.
Do they speak fluent ancient truths?
Or just seek the flashlight's light?

And in the garden, gnomes convene,
Exchanging secrets by the roses.
What do they know of time and space?
Or is it merely gossip that poses?

When Questions Dance with Answers

Why is the sky so vast and blue?
Do clouds gather for a comedy show?
Or maybe they're hiding from the sun,
In a game of tag, we don't know.

Every tick-tock whispers a thought,
Chasing shadows through the day.
Are clocks just jesters in disguise?
Making time laugh as it frays?

Do ants have parties underground?
Or do they solve puzzles of old?
Each crumb a treasure they hoard tight,
While we humans just watch, uncontrolled.

When the moon grins like a Cheshire cat,
Does it wink at the stars up high?
Is night just nature's punchline,
That makes us laugh till we cry?

The Riddle of Tomorrow's Dawn

Morning whispers in shades of gold,
Is it a secret or a sigh?
The sun steals kisses from the earth,
With a wink that nudges the sky.

What lies beneath the ocean's waves?
A kingdom of fish in disguise?
Or perhaps a mermaid's lost sock,
And turtles wearing their wise ties?

Why do dreams seem so absurd?
Like juggling jelly on a train?
Is it a plot by the mind's actors,
To keep us guessing insane?

Tomorrow's riddle spins anew,
Will answers ever take their stance?
Or must we dance in circles still,
Like kids lost in a silly prance?

Puzzles Wrapped in Stardust

Stars are just dots on a giant coat,
Wondering who's the tailor of fate.
Do they giggle when they twinkle bright?
Or sigh softly as they await?

Why do rainbows smile after rain?
Is it nature's own joke played well?
Or the sun trying out new crayons,
With colors too bright to quell?

Do trees have stories in their rings?
Of squirrels who dreamed to fly?
Or whispers of breezes long gone,
Floating tales that flutter by?

If shadows chuckle in the night,
What secrets do they find at dawn?
Life's a grand riddle, don't you think?
With laughter as our favorite song.

Where Clarity Dares to Tread

In the land of socks lost, we wander,
Searching for answers, yet we ponder.
Why do toasters always burn bread?
Maybe those crumbs just want to be fed.

Elusive truths, like cats that roam,
Chasing shadows, but never at home.
Why do we park on driveways, you see?
Perhaps the world loves its own irony.

Frogs in tuxedos sing in the rain,
Maybe they're pondering love's sweet pain.
What makes the moon cheese, or so they say?
Just a snack for a cow on a holiday.

Oh, the fun of questions that twirl and sway,
Like a whirlwind of thoughts on a sunny day.
In the pursuit of wisdom, we laugh and we cheer,
For answers are fickle, yet we still hang near.

The Language of Questions

Why do we always chase our own tail?
It's a riddle as old as the nighttime whale.
What makes the clock tick, or so it seems?
Just a way to mess with our wildest dreams.

What do clouds whisper when they're high?
Secrets to the birds that soar and fly.
Why do we ask the same things each day?
Perhaps our brains like to play a game of 'Say'.

Do fish really know they're underwater?
Or do they just think it's a life-long charter?
Why does ketchup struggle to pour?
A bottle of secrets, it holds at its core.

The joy of questioning, a dance of the mind,
In the waltz of confusion, together we find.
For answers elude us, but oh what a quest,
In this merry chase, we are truly blessed.

Fractured Truths

What's the deal with socks in the dryer?
They vanish like dreams caught in a fire.
Do left shoes conspire with old rubber bands?
Or is it the dust bunnies, forming strange bands?

Why do we lose keys right under our nose?
Probably the gremlins, I suppose.
What makes the fridge hum such a tune?
An ode to leftovers and cold afternoon.

Why do we struggle to find our phones?
They mock us from couches, like kings on their thrones.
What's with all the 'hurry up' in our lives?
Maybe it's to outrun all the future drives.

In this quirky puzzle we often reside,
We laugh at ourselves, with nothing to hide.
For truths may be fractured, but joy is intact,
In the comedy of life, that's a simple fact.

The Allure of the Unfathomable

Why does the toaster always pop with a grin?
Is it laughing at us, or just feeling kin?
What draws us to mysteries wrapped in a bow?
Perhaps it's the thrill of not quite knowing how, you know?

What whispers to us from the depths of a book?
Characters live where our imaginations cook.
Why do we dance when the music's just right?
To waltz with the moon in the still of the night.

What makes the coffee so dark and divine?
Is it the beans or the sleep we decline?
Why do we giggle at shadows on walls?
Maybe they're just friends at our late-night calls.

In the dance of the ungraspable, we play,
With laughter and wonder, we chase night and day.
For all of the secrets that flutter and dart,
Are simply the puzzles that tickle the heart.

Reflections in a Broken Mirror

I looked at myself, what a sight!
A nose like a potato, hair out of fright.
Who knew that wisdom came with such quirks?
Just another day dodging fate's little jerks.

Mirrors can lie, or so they say,
Caught in a glance, I turned away.
With every crack, a new face appears,
Just like my life, fueled by laughter and tears.

Each piece of glass tells a tale,
Of my journey, half-blind, can't derail.
Wit's my armor, I wear it proud,
Dancing through doubt, standing loud.

So let's toast to the silly and strange,
Embracing the chaos, it's funny how we change.
In a broken reflection, I find my cheer,
Life's riddles solved with the right kind of beer.

Searching for Sense

I searched for answers in my sock drawer,
Found a missing sock and a whole lot more.
A relic of mornings where I'd lose my mind,
Chasing lost things, let's see what I find.

I pondered my choices over stale bread,
Wondered if ducks have ever felt dread.
Why do we veggie smoke instead of smoke meat?
Life has recipes that no chef can beat.

The cat looks wise, with his plotting gaze,
Perhaps he's the one who holds all the keys.
In this crazy puzzle, I'll scrap all my schemes,
For laughter and snacks are life's true dreams.

What's the sense in a sense that won't land?
Perhaps I should just take a nap instead.
With pillows of thoughts swirling in jive,
I'll laugh at the nonsense that keeps me alive.

Digging into the Dark

In the depths of the attic, I found a box,
Filled with past memories and a pair of socks.
A moldy sandwich from '93,
Told me that time has no sovereignty.

Old toys and trinkets, dust must be king,
Each tells a story, a forgotten fling.
Whispers of echoes from ages gone by,
What wisdom in clutter? I can only sigh.

Each cobweb moment is a chance to laugh,
Like a stand-up set on a flimsy path.
Digging through shadows, I trip on the light,
Find humor in chaos, it's a mighty delight.

So pass me the flashlight, I'm ready to roam,
Through mysteries packed in my childhood home.
With a heart full of giggles, I'll dig up the gold,
For even in darkness, life's tales unfold.

The Spectrum of Certainty

They say knowledge is power, I'm lost in the fray,
Spectrum of certainty picked up and tossed away.
I asked my goldfish for some insight,
He blinked with wisdom, and swam out of sight.

Colors of life, so vibrant and bold,
Yet my days often feel like retold.
Do socks know the travel of days and nights?
I'm certain they vanish, but who starts the fights?

The universe giggles; it plays with our heads,
Certainty's just a myth, like my unmade beds.
With laughter, I'll chase every doubt to its end,
Life's jumbles and puzzles are better with friends.

So let us toast to the wise and the woeful,
To the riddles we'll face, to the playful and hopeful.
In this rainbow of nonsense, we'll find our way,
And dance in the chaos, come what may!

Breadcrumbs to Epiphanies

In a quest for truth, I made a trail,
With crumbs of insights, I set my sail.
Each slice of wisdom, a snack for thought,
But butterflies ate them, now I'm distraught.

I pondered why socks vanish into air,
While searching for answers, I found a bear.
It didn't know either, shrugged with a grin,
Now our deep conversations start to begin.

I sketched a map of my winding mind,
Every roadblock, a treasure to find.
But every route led to a pie in the sky,
Now I'm pie-sitting, oh my, oh my!

Yet I trudge on, with humor in tow,
For life's little puzzles have their own flow.
Between giggles and gaffes, joy lights the way,
Who knew breadcrumbs could lead me astray?

Fragments of Forgotten Dreams

I once dreamed of flying, like birds, so free,
But woke up to find a cat on my knee.
Was it deep insight or just a fluff ball?
In the maze of my sleep, I seem to stall.

I chased after starlight, you know, for a while,
Thought I might float on an ethereal smile.
But the stars just giggled, as I leaped and tripped,
Now I'm stargazing, with dream sheets equipped.

Midnight revelations drift in on a breeze,
With whispers of wonders that make my head tease.
But when morning light hits, they're gone like a flash,
Only fragments remain, a nostalgic clash.

Yet I treasure those moments, both wild and odd,
In the gallery of dreams, I'm both artist and fraud.
With laughter, I paint away shadows, and schemes,
Grateful for all of those forgotten dreams.

The Art of Half-Answers

Why does the toast always land with a thud?
I asked the universe, it just gave me a shrug.
Are socks more sneaky when paired at the gym?
Or maybe they're plotting a takeover on a whim?

I sought the great answer to life's silly games,
But all I found was a cat chasing flames.
Now I'm left pondering if wisdom's a joke,
Or just an illusion—another hoax stroke.

Why do our dreams love to hide in plain sight?
Are they just shy, or preparing for flight?
I grabbed my old questions and tossed them around,
But only half-answers in chaos I found.

So I laugh with the questions, embrace the absurd,
For the fun in the search is the strangest word.
Life's just a riddle with sideshows and clowns,
And half of my answers wear silly hats and gowns.

Journeys through the Unknown

I packed my bags for an unknown quest,
With snacks and some quips, I felt quite blessed.
The map said 'Adventure' on every page,
But I tripped on my shoelace, the first stage.

I stumbled through woods where the shadows creak,
Chatting with trees that felt oddly sleek.
"Do you have the answers?" I playfully asked,
They rustled their leaves, but wisdom hid masked.

Next stop was a hill where the wild winds blew,
Where I pondered deep questions without any clue.
Like why do the ducks always waddle in line?
With no answers at hand, I just laughed and felt fine.

So here's to the journeys, the laughs we will find,
Through all of the turns and the twists of the mind.
In the heart of confusion lies giggles and cheer,
And joy in the unknown, let's give it a cheer!

Searching for the Elusive Clarity

I looked for answers 'neath my bed,
Found only dust bunnies and dread.
The universe chuckles, isn't it grand?
Perhaps my confusion was all just a plan.

Toasters toast bread, but not my thoughts,
Where did I put the insights I sought?
A cat thinks it's wise with its sly little purr,
While I'm left to ponder, was I meant to stir?

I asked my goldfish about life's great quest,
It swam in circles; I'd say it knows best.
Mysteries float like bubbles, they rise,
Pop! There goes the truth, much to my surprise.

If laughter is wisdom, then I must be sage,
Each riddle I solve seems to fit on a page.
So here's to the chaos, the giggles and grins,
In the search for the meaning, let the comedy win.

Beyond the Veil of Perception

My glasses are fogged; nothing gets through,
Is that a squirrel or a myth I drew?
Reality winks with a mischievous twirl,
While I'm just here, lost in a whirl.

The stars tell tales of ancient delight,
But at midnight, I stumble – it's quite the sight.
I asked the shadows if they had a clue,
They just giggled and danced, as shadows do.

In the garden of wisdom, weeds seem to sprout,
What's real and what's fancy, who figures that out?
If perception is king, I've missed the decree,
Caught in a riddle, just sipping my tea.

So here's to confusion, the fun and the flair,
Laughter's the lens that I wear, I swear.
With logic around me, a circus of thought,
We'll juggle the nonsense – the wisdom I sought.

Fragments of the Unsolved

I found a puzzle with missing a piece,
Maybe my life feels like this, at least.
A clue in the cookie, I started to munch,
But all I got was a crumb-filled lunch.

The map was marked, but led to a wall,
My compass is wonky, it spins and it stalls.
I wrote down my dreams, but it made no sense,
As if logic got lost in some high-tech fence.

With every answer, a question was bred,
Is coffee or tea what's fueling my head?
Each fragment of wisdom shakes like a leaf,
A humorous dance in the garden of grief.

So here's to the pieces that stubbornly hide,
And laughter that lingers just over the tide.
In fragments we wander, through jests and through jibes,
Unsolved is the glory, our fun-loving vibes.

The Underbelly of Normalcy

There's a pattern in chaos, or so they proclaim,
But my socks are mismatched, it's driving me insane.
In the realm of routine, absurdity gleams,
And I wake from my dreams tangled up in my seams.

Grocery lists laden with things I forgot,
Did I need ice cream, or a big rubber yacht?
Normal it seems is just what we wear,
Like a t-shirt that says, 'I'm too cool to care.'

In the mirror, I see a familiar face,
Yet in my reflection, there's a strange embrace.
It winks and it curls in a humorous dance,
Making mischief out of life's silly chance.

So let's toast to the mundane and all that it yields,
There's magic in chaos, laughter repields.
The underbelly of normalcy, quirky and bright,
Turns life into jest; we'll laugh into the night.

Unmasking the Ordinary

In the fridge, what lies within,
A half-used pickle jar, a secret sin.
The cat stares deep, with wisdom galore,
What does he know? Oh, we'd love to explore.

The sock that vanished, where did it flee?
Hiding with its mate, under the TV.
A search begins, chaos reigns supreme,
The couch is a portal; oh, what a dream!

Everyday wonders, like toast that won't pop,
A puzzle of life with each burn and each flop.
We laugh and we sigh as crumbs scatter 'round,
In this grand circus, joy's always found.

The car keys lost, a regular spree,
They were on my head? Oh, how can this be?
Each fleeting moment, a tickle and tease,
In the game of the mundane, we find our ease.

Secrets Whispers in the Dark

The shadows chuckle, secrets they keep,
Why do we trip? Was it the darkness that creeps?
In corners they giggle, behind the bookcase,
Why does dust bunnies always seem to race?

Under the bed, what lurks in the night?
A spider's ballet, a hilarious sight.
With eight little legs, it twirls and it dip,
Chasing off nightmares, it leads quite a trip.

The closet's a tale of forgotten old shoes,
Each with its story, each one has a muse.
Do they plot together? They surely must plan,
To reunite with feet, once again to stand.

The clock strikes twelve, the world holds its breath,
Is it a silhouette or a shadow of death?
Yet, in the stillness, a chuckle or two,
Life's little dramas always feel so askew.

The Dance of Understanding

In the kitchen, the pots have a ball,
They bang and they clatter, they dance down the hall.
The pan takes the lead, with a sizzle and spin,
A culinary party, let the fun begin!

The toaster joins in, pops up with a cheer,
A slice of good bread and all we hold dear.
In rhythm we toast, in sync we engage,
Every morning a show on the breakfast stage!

Chores turn to waltzes, a mop takes a spin,
Vacuum's the DJ, it's chaos within.
As we hum to the beat, we dance through our day,
Finding joy in the hustle, come what may.

Laundry's a jig, as socks tumble and fling,
Oh, the mysteries held in this domestic swing!
Life is a party, in every sweet glance,
We twirl through the troubles, this wild, silly dance.

Beneath the Layers of Knowing

Papery onions shed tears of despair,
Each layer unpeeled, brings giggles to share.
What's hidden inside, just scents and some tears,
Yet come dinnertime laughter, it'll rob us of fears.

Paper cuts whisper, as they silently sing,
A cautionary tale of the joy that they bring.
Beneath every mishap, humor's always near,
Even in moments that seem rather drear.

A jogger's fall leads to an impromptu show,
A tumble, a trip, laughter starts to flow.
With every slip, we roll on the ground,
In the theater of life, hilarity found!

Each puzzle of knowledge, a riddle to crack,
We stumble, we giggle, and then we get back.
Behind every thought, a chuckle awaits,
In this grand experiment, laughter's the fates.

www.ingramcontent.com/pod-product-compliance
Lightning Source LLC
Chambersburg PA
CBHW051643160426
43209CB00004B/772